PRA
THE EN

C000275638

PRAYING WITH

The
English
Mystics

Compiled and introduced by
Jenny Robertson

TRIANGLE

First published 1990
Triangle
SPCK
Holy Trinity Church
Marylebone Road
London NW1 4DU

Second impression 1997

British Library Cataloguing in Publication Data
Praying with the English mystics.
  1. Christian life. Prayers – Devotional works
  I. Robertson, Jenny
  242′.8

ISBN 0-281-04454-6

Typeset by Rowland Phototypesetting Ltd
Bury St Edmunds, Suffolk
Printed and bound in Great Britain by
Caledonian International Book Manufacturing Ltd, Glasgow

Contents

Introduction

Prayer takes many forms. It may be private and personal. It may be a gesture, a breathing in, a sigh, a simple lifting of our heart and mind to God. Prayer may be silent or spoken. It may be entirely without words. Prayer may fill us with happiness, joy or peace, or we may be left feeling emptier than before. Prayer may lead us into barrenness, into a desert place, or into what St John of the Cross, who lived in Spain in the sixteenth century, called 'the dark night of the soul'.

Prayer takes us on a pilgrimage into ourselves and out to our neighbour, and this seems to be exactly what God intends, for throughout the Bible, through the Psalms and the prophets, the birth of Christ, his death and resurrection, the gift of the Spirit and the life of the Church, the Creator comes into creation, is made one with seed, cornstalk and sheepfold, birthing, hunger and pain; experiences rejection and failure; goes without food or sleep; goes to parties, feasts. And the one who comes, invites us: Come.

Come, be a child. God offers us this closest, most intimate relationship, and all through his time on earth Jesus will embody the loving, trusting relationship which his birth as a naked child so completely symbolises.

But for Jesus, being a child of the Father meant becoming a slave. We learn from Paul's epistle that slaves might live in the household with the children, but they would never inherit the father's wealth. Inheritance belonged only to those who were children by blood or adoption.

Jesus becomes a slave so that we might enter into our full inheritance.

The first Christians understood this very well and were astounded by it. They sang:

He always had the nature of God,
    but . . . of his own free will
        he gave up all he had,
        and took the nature of a servant.

(Philippians 2.6, 7, GNB)

In the same way Lady Julian of Norwich sees God as Creator of all that is made (*Showings*, 5), loving and serving us so totally that 'soul and body' we are 'clad and enclosed in the goodness of God'.

It is exactly this calling of love, the intimate relationship of trust in the one who comes, who invites us: Come, which each of the four fourteenth-century English writers, who are called 'mystics', reflect on in their prayers. I have drawn upon their writings to compile this book. I am not a theologian, nor a historian, nor am I expert in prayer (is anyone?). I do not lead retreats, I do not lead anything. I was a social worker once, and in this way I tried to take compassion into people's lives (but my own was just as muddled and just as much in need of understanding). I looked after my growing children and a totally handicapped parent for many long, slow years, and I had good cause to reflect upon the kinds of questions which these English writers also faced: Does prayer really work in the face of long-term suffering? And how can a God of love allow pain?

These questions took me, as they took the fourteenth-century writers, as they take us all, to the heart of God: to the Passion of Christ. This is, quite simply, the greatest story ever told. It hushes unruly children to stillness. It turns criminals into lovers. It has been the theme of everything that is greatest and best in art, music and story. It is, of course, the theme and the core of Christian worship, and there has been a long tradition of depicting the life of the Lord, his sufferings, death and resurrection. In centuries when books were rare, every church was its own visual aid. Its very shape was cruciform and its frescos and carvings retold the story in which worshippers were involved.

Thus it was that the details of the life of Jesus of Nazareth were as familiar to a medieval child as the doings of the latest TV soap are to children today. The medieval mind was so profoundly immersed in the Passion of Christ that kings would walk barefoot and wash their subjects' feet. Surrounded by images of the naked Christ, our four mystics found the riches of heaven revealed.

So the unknown author of the spiritual classic, *The Cloud of Unknowing* writes:

> Lord God, you fit yourself exactly to our souls
> by adapting your Godhead to them . . .
> *Cloud of Unknowing*, 4

The troubled fourteenth century, a time of tremendous disaster, change and unrest, was rich in spiritual explorers whose names and works are still familiar today. Walk into twentieth-century bookshops and you will still find copies of *The Cloud of Unknowing*, Walter Hilton's *Ladder of Perfection*, the writings of the Yorkshire hermit Richard Rolle and, perhaps best known and loved of them all, Lady Julian of Norwich. That is not bad going! These authors of books with a shelf life of six hundred years compete easily in a market where some books last a bare six weeks. In Western Europe, too, were other great women and men of prayer whose work has nurtured

Christian hearts for centuries, not least Thomas à Kempis. Deeply earthed in the dangers and difficulties of a troubled age, these people of prayer worked against a background of a Church torn in two by a divided Papacy. The emergence of nationalism and various vernaculars gave rise to ideas which threatened the structure of Christendom, while the Black Death decimated whole populations. War tore nations apart, and in England itself the early part of the century saw a royal scandal which led to the abdication and murder of the king, while later years saw the stirrings of social unrest in the Peasants' Revolt. And from this restless, unsettled century Lady Julian speaks to our own time: 'How could anything be amiss?' for, 'All will be well, and all will be well, and every kind of thing will be well.' (*Showings*, 11, 27), while Richard Rolle adds, 'May God's cheerfulness forever sing out merrily in your life.' ('Ghostly Gladness')

All four writers show sensitivity and good counsel in their works. They were well used to offering spiritual direction. Walter Hilton's *Ladder of Perfection* was written specifically as a guide to prayer for a woman, an anchoress. Richard Rolle's English Writings include *The Form of Living*, a letter of spiritual direction written with tact and humour to a woman, Margaret Kirkby, whom he helped through an epileptic attack. The unknown author of *The Cloud of Unknowing* is thought to have been a spiritual director, and *The Cloud* is clearly intended for a young Christian whom God is calling to 'gaze at him, and leave him to act alone'. (*Cloud*, 2). Julian of Norwich herself, although enclosed as an anchoress, offered advice and help to at least one other woman, Margery Kempe, who describes in her *Book* discussions with Lady Julian which proved of great spiritual benefit to illiterate Margery.

Indeed, Walter Hilton's instructions to his anchoress show that a woman who chose the life of prayer, shut away in a house she would never leave until her death, might be very much distracted by constant interruptions. And, advised Walter Hilton, the anchoress should find God in this stranger just as much as in prayer, for God is present in our neighbour, and the secret of the life of prayer is 'to be continually at prayer' (*Ladder* I, 83, 32); while Richard Rolle, who gave up his studies at Oxford to become a hermit, found that his love for God finally brought his unsocial soul peace with his neighbour: 'You have made us so that to love and be loved is the delightful purpose of our human life.' (*Fire of Love*, 25).

Chronologically, Richard Rolle is the first of the four English mystics whose prayers make up this book. He is thought to have been born around 1300 in Thornton-le-Dale, near Pickering in North Yorkshire. As a young man of nineteen he left Oxford and plunged dramatically into the life of a hermit, vandalising two of his sister's gowns in order to make himself a tunic. He prudently, however, sought the help of local gentry who kitted him out with rough clothing and supplied him with some sort of shelter. These details of Rolle's life were recorded in 1380 in preparation for his canonisation which never in fact took place, but he inspired a flourishing cult, particularly among the poor, and among women, for whom he wrote his later 'English writings'. Ecstatic, lyrical outpourings of devotion and love for Jesus in ornate Latin describe Rolle's mystical experiences, although he acknowledges that this 'inexpressible joy' of God's love can never be described; to do so would be 'like trying to empty the sea'. (*Fire*, 34). Music bubbling up from a heart filled with praise, warmth which is physically felt, were part of Rolle's experience. He felt himself to be 'like the nightingale who pines for her love' (see page 16) singing and yearning all night long. And he prays:

> How much more, Christ my Jesu,
> ought I to sing to you,
> spouse of my soul,
> through all this present life
> which is night for me now
> compared with the brightness to come.

Richard Rolle's love of the Name of Jesus links him firmly with the Eastern Orthodox, with their long tradition of the Jesus Prayer. Within the English tradition his meditative prayer, deeply imbued with Scripture, links him with St Anselm, while his English writings provide the groundwork for the other three writers in this book, who also chose to express their love of God not in the Latin of the learned, nor in the Norman French of courtly dalliance, but in the native English of the emerging middle classes, the speech, too, of women and of the poor.

It is likely that Richard Rolle, Christ's nightingale, died in the Black Death which emptied courtyard and cloister in the fourteenth century. He left a rich legacy of spiritual guidance, but some of his more ecstatic writings were misinterpreted. *The Cloud of Unknowing*, written probably around 1370, sought to play down physical manifestations of the presence of God, and, with Walter Hilton, its unknown author anticipates the path which would later be explored by the Spanish mystics, John of the Cross and Teresa of Avila, charting the progress of the soul to union with God. It is thought that the writer of *The Cloud* came from the East Midlands, where he may have been a priest and a spiritual director. His teachings emphasise the 'otherness' of God, who can be known by love and prayer which leads through the intellectual darkness of 'the cloud of unknowing'. There is much sane guidance in this man's teachings, and much that is helpful for Christians today, especially his emphasis on 'a simple reaching out directly towards God' by means of 'just a little word . . . the shorter it is the better'. The 'arrow' prayers in this book are derived from this teaching. This author's faith speaks to our times in his quiet confidence:

> You, by yourself alone,
> and no one but you,
> are fully sufficient,
> and much more so,
> to fulfill the will and desire
> of our souls.
>
> (*Cloud*, 4)

Walter Hilton, a monk giving spiritual advice to an anchoress, wrote a book which continues to offer deep teaching on the stages of prayer, and has something in common with a later English classic, *Pilgrim's Progress*, being a delightful allegory of the pilgrim's path towards the heavenly Jerusalem. But the pilgrim needs food and refreshment on the way, a good inn and good companionship, and God similarly helps us in our dryness and barrenness. *The Ladder of Perfection* has plenty to offer to twentieth-century minds who experience depression and dryness, who look for knowledge which, says Hilton, by itself is 'like water, tasteless and cold,' but by the gift of the Holy Spirit 'this savourless knowledge' turns 'into wisdom . . . spiritual light and burning love.' (*Ladder*, I, 4)

Walter Hilton also anticipates John of the Cross in describing his experience of the 'dark night of the soul'.

But this is a night pregnant with good,
 a glowing darkness,
for it shuts out the false love of the world,
and ushers in the dawn of your true day.
Indeed, the darker the night,
the nearer the true day of your love . . .
When I sit in darkness, the Lord is my light.
         (*Ladder* II, 24)

This is wise teaching for those whose path of prayer seems dark, and Hilton's trust that 'You are in the darkness, whether it brings pain or peace' (p. 70) is a real guideline for many people who are reaching out to God in the midst of pain.

Similarly, Julian of Norwich wrestles with the 'problem of pain', trying to square suffering on this earth (and the hell which she knows Holy Church teaches) with her vision of the love of God and her certainty that 'all shall be well'. Julian is known today for one book, *Showings*, a two-part account of a vision granted to her when she was thirty of the love of God experienced in the sufferings of Christ. In her youth Julian prayed for three things: first a deep understanding of Christ's Passion, 'so that I might have suffered with him as others did that love him'. She asked also for a physical illness, 'every kind of pain, bodily and spiritual, which I should have had if I had died', but, since that was an unusual prayer, Julian added 'if it be your will, good Lord'; and then, 'by the grace of God and the teaching of Holy Church', Julian wanted three wounds: 'true contrition . . . loving compassion and the wound of longing with my will for God' (*Showings*, Long Text, 2).

Far from being a morbid desire for suffering, perhaps as a sort of self-promotion, Julian's request shows great insight and moral integrity. Like the other writers, Julian is aware that true personhood and healing is found only when we are rooted in God. The truth is that when we contemplate Jesus in his need we learn kindness for ourselves and for others. And when with our whole being we enter the death of Jesus, we can find our true at-one-ment which reconciles us to pain and joy, for we learn, as Julian does, that 'love was his meaning'.

In May 1373, when she was thirty years old, Julian, ill and on the point of death, received a vision of the dying Christ. She recovered from her illness, and soon after wrote the first part of her *Showings*, reflecting on this experience. Julian became an anchoress, and probably takes her name from the church of St Julian, beside which she was enclosed, able to look through a window at the services in church, and hear the hustle and bustle of the Norwich streets. Twenty years after receiving the visions she expanded the short text of her *Showings* into a book which has enriched friends and lovers of Christ for centuries.

Julian's writings, and the works of the other three writers, are adapted here as short prayers which can be used by individuals or by groups. Some are simply 'arrow prayers', others are rather more meditative; some are rooted in praise and thanksgiving; and there are sections on the Passion of Christ, on contrition and confession, as well as on the experience of darkness. Julian, delighting in the sensual, attuned to the love of God in every aspect of creation, develops ideas of the mothering, nurturing aspects of the Holy Trinity. In this she is following a long biblical tradition, from Exodus through Isaiah and Hosea, and also the writings of Christians such as St Anselm of Canterbury and Walter de Thierry. So there are prayers here on the Motherhood of God, and the book is rounded off with blessings from each of the writers, who in

troubled times found such peace in loving God
that their words provide counsel and comfort
today:

> I beseech almighty God
> that true peace, sane counsel,
> and spiritual comfort in God,
> with abundance of grace,
> be always with you
> and with all those on earth who love God.

(Cloud, 75)

THE SONG OF YOUR PRAISING

That I may praise you worthily

To you, O God,
every heart stands open,
and every will speaks;
no secret is hidden from you.
Purify my mind,
my thoughts and my heart
with the gift of your grace,
so that I may love you perfectly
and praise you worthily.

Cloud, Prologue

Almighty Creator

Blessed be you, Lord,
divinity, who always was, and is, and shall be,
    almighty, all wisdom and all love;
everything you have made,
heaven and earth and all creation
is great and generous
and beautiful and good,
for you created everything for love,
and by your love it is preserved,
and always will be, without end.
Lord, you are everything which is good,
and the goodness which is in everything
    is yourself, our God.

Julian, *Showings*, 8

4

The greatest possible joy

Lord Jesus,
it is the greatest possible joy
that you are highest and mightiest,
noblest and most honourable,
    lowest and humblest,
most familiar and courteous.
And truly you will show us
all this marvellous joy
    when we shall see you.
And you want us to believe this
and trust, rejoice and delight,
strengthen and console ourselves,
as we can, with your grace and help,
until the time that we see it in reality.
For the greatest abundance of joy
    which we shall have,
is this wonderful courtesy
and familiarity of our Father,
    who is our Creator,
in you, our Lord Jesus Christ,
    our brother and our saviour.

Julian, *Showings*, 7

The sound of praising

Song is the great happiness
of thinking of eternal things
and of eternal joy
breaking out in the sound of praising.
So may we love you, our God,
with a cheerful mood.
Fill our souls with rejoicing and tenderness,
so that we may praise you
not only in the heart
but with the voice also.

Rolle, Prologue to *Psalter*

I want to praise you always

I want to give you, my God, unceasing praise.
You comfort me when I am in trouble;
when success crowns my work
you show me how to await with confidence
your everlasting prize.

Jesus, I want to be praising you always,
such is my joy.

Rolle, *Fire*, 15

I love you for being yourself

It is good to think of your kindness, O God,
and to love you and praise you for that.
Yet it is far better to think upon
    your simple being,
and to love you and praise you
    for yourself.

Cloud, 5

Jesu, my joying

Praised be you, my king,
and thanked be you, my king,
and blessed be you, my king,
   Jesu, all my joying,
of all your gifts most good;
who for me spilled your blood,
and died upon the rood;
    now give me grace to sing
    the song of your praising.

Rolle, *The Form of Living*, 7

All I need

My God,
you are all I need, and more;
whoever has you needs nothing else
   in this life.

MY ONLY DESIRE

You alone I desire

Lord Jesus Christ,
I lift up to you my mind
and my heartfelt desire,
even though I am blind
and can see nothing of your Godhead.
It is you whom I have lost,
and you alone whom I desire to have,
that I may be with you where you are,
since there is no other joy,
no other bliss
in heaven or in earth,
except in you.

Hilton, *Ladder*, I, 46

You alone are heaven

What is heaven to me, Lord?
Surely it is nothing other
   than Jesus my God.
For if heaven is that
   which is above all things,
then, Lord God, you alone
   are heaven to my soul.

Hilton, *Ladder*, II, 33

Dearest of all most sweet

Jesus, your love is the dearest
　　of all that is most sweet!
You take hold of our minds
　　with your love;
you possess us so clearly
because you make us despise
　　all transitory things,
and yearn marvellously
　　for what you desire.
You came to me,
and every corner of my heart
has been filled with the lovely sound
of your joy.

Rolle, *Fire*, 16

The nightingale

When first I turned to you, my Jesus,
I thought I would be
like the nightingale who pines for her love,
and rejoices in the midst of her longing
when the loved one comes.
While she sings her joy, she is still yearning,
though in sweetness and warmth.
The nightingale will sing all night long
to please her beloved.
How much more, Christ my Jesu,
ought I to sing to you,
spouse of my soul,
through all this present life
which is night for me now
compared with the brightness to come.

Rolle, *Fire*, 42

My God and my comfort

There is delightful warmth in my heart
now you have filled me with your love.
This fiery, burning love
has consumed gloom and trouble,
and from it issues sweetness
and in particular, music
which soothes my soul,
for there, my God and my comfort,
you have set up your Temple.

Rolle, *Fire*, 42

May I love your name, Jesus

I appeal to you, Lord,
that, as I yearn to be your lover,
I may love your name, JESUS,
and meditate on it in my heart,
so that I may never forget it
wherever I am.
I shall find great joy and strength
in your name, Lord Jesus,
and because I love you so tenderly,
and as such an intimate friend,
you will fill me with grace on this earth
greater than I know how to wish for.
Your goodness is so great
that when we request only one of something
    you will give us three,
so very pleased are you when we decide
to direct our whole heart to love you.

Rolle, *Ego Dormio*

Set ablaze by your love

Jesus,
enlightened by your grace,
and set ablaze by the fire of your love,
I truly feel the burning of love in my heart,
constantly lifting my mind towards God,
filling me with love, joy and sweetness,
so that no illness, nor mental agony,
nor humiliation, nor harsh living conditions
are able to distress me,
because you have changed my whole life to joy.
You have lifted up my heart
so that my prayers turn into joyful song
    and my thoughts into sweet sounds.
Now, Jesus, you are all my desire,
    all my delight, all my joy,
all my consolation, all my strength
    so that my song will always be of you,
and in you all my rest.

Rolle, *Ego Dormio*

Your will is to possess us

God, our Lover,
you desire the soul
to adhere to you with all its power
and you want us always
to adhere to your goodness.
For of all things
    that the heart can think,
this pleases you most
and soonest profits the soul,
    so preciously loved.
So, with reverence,
we ask from you, our Lover,
all that we will,
for our natural will
is to possess you, God,
and your good will
is to possess us.

Julian, *Showings*, 6

Love, God's own darling

Jesu, who to me life lent, into your love me bring:
To you take my whole intent, for you be all my
 longing.
Woe would away from me be sent, done would be all
 my wanting
If but my soul hear and consent to the song of your
 praising.

Love is a light burden, love gladdens young and old,
Love is without all pain, as lovers have me told;
Love is a holy wine, which makes us brave and bold.
Love shall no jot decline once we in heart it hold.

Love is the sweetest thing that we on earth have
 known;
Love is God's own darling; love binds by blood and
 bone.
In love be our liking, I know not a better home;
For me and my loving, by love we're both made one.

Rolle, *Lyrics*

Jesu, my love-longing

Hail Jesu, my Creator, of suffering the cure;
Hail Jesu, my Saviour, for me suffering torture;
Hail Jesu, help and succour, to you love I assure;
Hail Jesu, blessed flower of maiden mother pure.

Hail Jesu, leader to light, in soul you are most sweet;
Your love shines both day and night, which
    strengthens me on this street.
Lend me longing for your sight, and give me grace to
    weep;
For you, Jesu, have the might my sorrows away to
    sweep.

Jesu, with grace my heart inspire, to bliss may it me
    bring;
On you I place all my desire, you are my
    love-longing;
Your love is burning like the fire which ever up will
    spring;
Far from me put pride and anger: for them I've no
    loving.

Rolle, *Lyrics*

The nail of love

Lord Jesus Christ,
summon together all the desires of my soul
and fasten them to you with the nail of love
so that even one hour of one day
would seem too long to be away from you,
since I long continually for you.

Rolle, *Psalm 12*

You have enslaved me

Your love, Lord, has laid hold of my heart.
You have bound, enslaved and entwined me
with such vigour and wonderful mastery
that I would rather die than live.
Your flower of love, Jesus, will never wither,
for you, my friend, are so ardent in love
that you fuse together death and joy and song.

Rolle, *Fire*, 42

Trying to empty the sea

Jesus,
the delightful taste of your love
is impossible to describe.
If I were wanting to speak about
your inexpressible joy, Lord Jesus,
I would seem to be trying to empty the sea
    drop by drop,
and bit by bit to squeeze it
into a tiny hole in the sand.

Rolle, *Fire*, 34

Jesu my joy

When will you come, Jesu my joy, to reprieve me
    from care,
Yourself give to me, for me to see, living evermore?
All my desiring had come if I were with you there.
I want no thing save only you; my one wish I declare.

Rolle, 'A Song of Love', *Ego Dormio*

The love of your loving

I know no better weal
than in my heart to feel
the love of your loving.
Of all it is the best
to hold you, Jesus, firmest
and crave no other thing.

Rolle, *Psalm 61*

Arrow Prayers

When will you come, Jesus, my joy?

Rolle, Song of Love

Jesus, truly my treasure is you.

Rolle, Fire, 16

I have found Jesus, my Love.

Rolle, Fire, 27

To love you only, Jesus, and find joy in you alone:
this is my prayer.

Rolle, Fire, 36

Lord, I covet you and seek you and nothing but you.

Cloud, 7

CREATOR AND REDEEMER

In your love is our beginning

Lord God,
before you made us
you loved us;
your love was never abated,
and never will be.
And in your love
   you have done all your works,
and in your love
   you have made all things profitable to us,
and in your love
   our life is everlasting.
In our creation
   we had our beginning,
but the love in which you created us
was in you from without beginning.
In your love
we have our beginning,
and all this shall we see
in you, Lord God without end.
Thanks be to God.

Julian, *Showings*, 86

We are clad in your goodness

Lord God,
you come down to us in our humblest needs.
You do not despise what you have made,
or disdain to serve us
in the simplest natural functions of our body,
for you love the soul which you created
in your own likeness.
For as the body is clad in the cloth,
and the flesh in the skin,
and the bones in the flesh,
and the heart in the trunk
so are we, body and soul,
clad and enclosed in your goodness,
O God.

Julian, *Showings*, 6

32

You fit yourself to our souls

Lord God,
you fit yourself exactly to our souls
by adapting your Godhead to them;
and our souls are fitted exactly to you
by the worthiness of our creation
after your image and in your likeness.
You, by yourself alone,
and no one but you,
are fully sufficient,
and much more so,
to fulfill the will and the desire
    of our souls.
Your reforming grace
enables our soul
to comprehend you by love
in all your entirety.

Cloud, 4

A leash of longing

Lord,
in your great mercy you called me
and led me to you
by the desire you put in my heart.
Your everlasting love
which made me and fashioned me
when I was nothing,
and bought me at the price
    of your precious blood,
when, in Adam, I was lost,
would not allow me to stray
    far from you.
And so, with your great grace
you kindled my desire,
and fastened it to a leash of longing
to be your servant.

Cloud, 1

A place of pasture

Almighty God,
King of Kings
and Lord of Lords,
it was your desire to humble yourself
to be on a level with us,
and out of the whole flock of your sheep
it was your will
   graciously to choose me
to be one of your special disciples.
You brought me into this place of pasture,
where I may be fed with the sweetness
   of your love;
and this is a pledge of my heritage,
the kingdom of heaven.

Cloud, 2

We fix you in our heart

Jesus, the best thing we can ever do
is to fix you in our heart,
and never want anything else.
We have made a good beginning
when we start to desire eternal things,
for you yearned for our love, Lord Christ,
when you hastened with such fervour
    to your cross to redeem us.
We truly say, 'Love precedes the dance,
    and gives the lead.'
It was nothing but love
which brought you down so low.

Rolle, *Fire*, 42

We are your crown

Lord Jesus, we are yours,
not only through our redemption,
but also by our Father's courteous gift.
We are your bliss,
we are your reward,
we are your honour,
we are your crown.

And this is a singular wonder,
and a most delectable contemplation,
that we are your crown.

Julian, *Showings*, 22

The humble stirring of love

Lord, I want to follow
   this humble stirring of love
which you put in my heart.
For you will be my guide
   in this life,
and bring me to grace
   in the next.
Your love in my heart
is the substance of all good living;
without your love
no good work can be begun or ended.
You direct my will to you
and you give me satisfaction and gladness
   concerning all that you do.

Cloud, 49

Mutual love

Lord God,
nothing is better than mutual love;
nothing is sweeter than holy charity.
You have so made us
that to love and to be loved
is the delightful purpose
of our human life,
the delight of your heavenly angels
and your most blessed reward.
For if we want to be loved,
we must simply love.
Love gets love in return.
Thank you that no one has ever lost
    through loving;
though we will never know how to rejoice
until we know what it is to burn with love;
for the greatness of your love, O God,
opens to us the sweet song
of everlasting praise.

Rolle, *Fire*, 25

The pilgrim's prayer

Lord,
I want to progress swiftly
along the road to your love,
and constantly to bear in mind two words,
humility and love.
Beside you, I am nothing,
and I want only one thing.
So help me to fix the true meaning
   of these words
for ever in my inner mind and purpose,
so that they will always guide me,
even when I do not think of them.
Humility says,
   'I am nothing, I have nothing.'
Love says,
   'I desire one thing only, which is Jesus.'
Touch these two strings with your finger, Lord,
and secure them by the thought of Jesus
to make sweet harmony
in the harp of my soul.

Hilton, *Ladder*, II, 21

The pilgrim's prayer continues . . .

Lord,
just as a pilgrim who travels all day
without eating or drinking
is nearly overcome by weariness,
but at last comes upon a good inn
and is well refreshed with food and drink,
so in the spiritual life
my soul wishes to renounce the love of the world
and love you, my God.
So I set myself to this,
but sometimes I pray and labour
in body and soul all day long
without feeling any comfort and joy.
Yet, Lord, you have pity on all your creatures
and you send me spiritual food
and comfort me with devotion as you see fit,
lest I perish, lose heart
or fall into depression and complaint.

Hilton, *Ladder*, II, 29

Loving God, we love our neighbour

Lord God,
make our love pure and perfect,
for then, whatever our heart loves
will be yourself, our God.
For in you we may love
everything you have made,
ourselves, your creation;
and what else are we doing
but loving you?
For when we love you
 with all our heart and mind,
undoubtedly we love our neighbour
and every other lovable thing.
So we would pour out to you
 our whole heart,
and by that token
you will bind us so closely to you
that we need no other love
 than yours.
For in your love, O God,
is the love of our neighbour also.

Rolle, *Fire*, 19

Serving our neighbour, we find God

Father,
if someone comes to see me while I am at prayer,
help me to see that
in leaving you to speak to this stranger,
I have not left you at all.
I will find you, possess you and see you
as fully in this other person
as I do when I am praying,
although it will be in a different way.

Hilton, *Ladder*, I, 83

You make your friends glad

You lifted my understanding up into heaven,
where I saw you, Lord God,
    as a lord in your house,
where you have called all your friends
    to a splendid feast.
You reign in your house as a king,
and fill it all full of joy and mirth.
You gladden and console your dear friends
    with yourself,
very familiarly and courteously,
with wonderful melody
in endless love
in your own fair blissful countenance,
and your glorious countenance
fills all heaven
full of your joy and bliss.

Julian, *Showings*, 14

44

The Giver is the Gift

Lord, I ask nothing of you
except the gift of your love,
   that is the Holy Spirit.
For among all your gifts
there is none so good and valuable
   so noble and excellent as this.
For in no other gift save your gift of Love
is the Giver himself the Gift,
so that this gift
is the noblest and best of all.

Hilton, *Ladder*, II, 36

May we love you and trust you

Lord Jesus,
it is your office to save us,
it is your glory to do it,
and it is your will that we know it.
May we love you sweetly
and trust in you meekly and greatly.

Julian, *Showings*, 61

LORD OF MERCY

I implore your mercy

Lord, who came down from heaven to earth
for love of the human race,
from so high to so low,
from such high dominion
   to such low poverty,
from such high magnificence
   to such low affliction,
from such high happiness
   to such low sorrow
from such a pleasurable life
   to such a painful death;
now, Lord, for all that love
which you revealed to mankind
in your incarnation
and in your passion,
I implore you for mercy and help.

Rolle, *Meditations on the Passion*

No pretence of holiness

Lord Jesus Christ,
make me wholly devoted to you.
Keep me, Lord God,
from making an outward show
    of conversion to you
without giving you my heart,
for that is only a shadow
    and pretence of virtue,
and no true conversion.
Help me to maintain inward vigilance,
and never make an outward show of holiness
    in dress, speech and behaviour;
nor watch the doings of other people
and criticise their faults,
imagining myself to be something,
when really I am nothing.
Help me to devote myself,
    soul and body
    to you alone,
shaping myself inwardly
    to your likeness
by humility, charity
    and other spiritual virtues.

Hilton, *Ladder*, I, 1

Give me your grace

Sweet Jesu, I implore you,
grant me grace to offer myself to you
   with my whole intent,
in heartfelt sorrow for my sins,
and calling out for mercy,
to reform myself in my motivation
by admitting my sins to you
   and doing penance for them,
by perseverance in virtuous living,
by total love for you who made me;
and allow me to turn to you
through frequent confession,
in every difficulty,
in every temptation of my body,
   of the world around me,
   or of the devil;
and bestow on me the grace
that every thought, word or act
   which emanates from me
may reveal that I am converted to you;
and give me grace
gladly to turn with full inclination
to those activities
   which you have appointed for me.
Sweet Jesu, Lord, I implore you,
hear my prayer.

Rolle, *Meditations on the Passion*

I desire your love

Lord, I desire your love,
not because I am worthy,
but because I am unworthy;
for if I had it,
it would make me worthy.
And since you created me for your love,
although I may never enjoy it,
I will still desire it,
pray for it
and hope to attain it.

Hilton, *Ladder*, II, 22

Always fresh and eager

Lord, who made me and all my limbs,
give me grace
to serve you with all my limbs
employed in your service,
constantly bending
   as you direct me,
constantly ready
   to move or rest at your command,
always immobilised
   to acts of sin,
always fresh and eager
   for your instructions.

Rolle, *Meditations on the Passion*

You are my heritage

Jesus, cast out all these sins from my heart.
Help me to sweep my soul clean
    with the broom of the fear of God,
and wash it with my tears,
and I shall find my lost coin,
    Jesus.
You are the coin,
you are the penny,
you are my heritage.

Hilton, *Ladder*, I, 48

54

I beg inwardly of Jesus

Lord,
I have acted in ways which shame,
so now I return to myself
   and remain there.
I will not wander abroad,
begging for the food of swine.
But I wish still to be a beggar,
and so I beg of you inwardly,
my Lord Jesus,
for you are rich indeed,
and you are more ready to give
   than I to ask.
You will supply all my wants.
You will take me to your cellar
and allow me to taste of your wines,
for you have many casks
   from which to choose.

Hilton, *Ladder*, I, 80

We may trust Christ to answer prayer

Lord Jesus,
you sleep spiritually in my heart
as once you slept bodily
in the ship with your disciples.
But they, fearing to perish,
awoke you,
and you quickly saved them from the tempest.
Therefore I will rouse you
    as they did, by prayer.
I will wake you with the loud cry
    of my desire,
and you will quickly rise
and help me.

Hilton, *Ladder*, I, 49

Fetch me home again

Sweet Jesu,
I implore you to lay hold on me
and make me entirely yours.
And if I should run off to any sin
caused by the world around me,
    my own body, or the devil,
sweet Jesu, fetch me straight home again,
as a lord does his serf,
and urge me on with hardship
    to immediate penance.
Sweet Jesu,
in you resides every sovereign remedy,
and I, Lord, am desperately ill with sins;
so take hold of me, sweet Jesu,
and place me under your treatment,
and move me close with your grace,
    as did the Samaritan,
and pour into my wounds
    the oil of forgiveness
    and the wine of invigoration,
and lead me into the shelter of love,
always keeping me under your treatment.

Rolle, *Meditations on the Passion*

A contaminated well

Lord Jesus, in my heart is a great evil,
a strong spring of self-love,
from which flow all kinds of sin.
And so I am like a man
who had in his garden a contaminated well
with many channels running from it.
He went and blocked these channels
but left the spring untouched,
thinking that all was now safe.
But the water sprung up
    at the bottom of the well
and stood stagnant for so long
that it ruined all the beauty of the garden,
although no water flowed out.
Your grace helps me to block
    the rivers of the spring,
but I want you to block and cleanse
the spring of evil within.
Unless you block it and cleanse it,
it will poison all the flowers
    in the garden of my soul,
however lovely they may outwardly appear
    to all who see them.

Hilton, *Ladder*, I, 55

I worship you in your gifts

Lord, who made me
and have given me many gifts,
spiritual, physical and material,
grant me grace
to use all of them in your service
and for the purpose
     for which you gave them to me,
so that I may constantly
     worship you in your gifts.
And grant me the grace
constantly to be humble
     in possessing your gifts,
and never to be presumptuous
     or proud of your gifts,
but constantly to recognise myself
     for what I am,
a sinful and worthless creature.

Rolle, *Meditations on the Passion*

To love you with all my wanting . . .

Lord, who made me like yourself,
give me the grace to love you
with all my soul,
with all my love,
with all my intention,
with all my pleasure,
with all my enjoyment,
with all my memory,
with all my wanting,
with all my devotion,
with all my longing,
with reforming of my life,
with all my desiring,
with enduring in virtue,
with contrition and confession to you
and penance for my sins.

Rolle, *Meditations on the Passion*

. . . *with all my activity,*
all my rest

Lord, who made me of nothing,
give me the grace to serve you
with all my heart,
with all my ability,
with all my strength,
with all my knowledge,
with all my endeavour,
with all my understanding,
with all the powers of my soul,
with all my attention,
with all my speech,
with all my senses,
with all my acts,
with all my employment,
with all my activity,
with all my rest.

Rolle, *Meditations on the Passion*

Wholehearted prayer

Lord, I want to pray with all my heart
even though it seems this has no savour to me;
it is profitable for me,
even though I may not feel it so.
I want to pray with all my heart
though I may feel nothing,
though I may see nothing,
yes, though I think I could not,
for in dryness and barrenness,
in sickness and in weakness,
my prayer is most pleasing to you,
though it is almost tasteless to me.
And so is all living prayer in your sight.

Julian, *Showings,* **41**

62

Look on me in mercy

Lord God, in your mercy
you do not look on what I am now
    nor on what I have been,
but on what I desire to be.

Cloud, 75

All will be well

Lord Jesus, I have heard you say:
'Sin is necessary
but all will be well,
and all will be well,
and every kind of thing
    will be well.'

Julian, *Showings*, 27

Arrow Prayers

Everything has being through your love, Lord God.

Julian, *Showings*, 5

God, of your goodness, give me yourself.

Julian, *Showings*, 5

Your goodness comes down to our humblest needs.

Julian, *Showings*, 6

You have grounded my soul deeply in you, God.
I am endlessly treasured.

Julian, *Showings*, 56

Help me now, for the love of Jesus.

Cloud, 4

Lord, you said: 'I protect you very surely.'

Julian, *Showings*, 37

Only pain blames and punishes.
Lord, you comfort and love us.
You bring us to your bliss.

Julian, *Showings*, 51

DARKNESS AND LIGHT

A cloud of unknowing

When I first begin to reach out to you, my God,
   all that I find is a darkness,
   a sort of cloud of unknowing;
I cannot tell what it is,
except I experience in my will
   a simple reaching out to you, Lord God.
This darkness is always between me and my God,
   no matter what I do,
and it prevents me from seeing you clearly
by the light of understanding in my reason,
and from experiencing you
in sweetness of love in my affection.
So help me to rest in this darkness
   as long as I can,
always crying out after you, whom I love.
For if I am to experience you
or to see you at all,
in so far as this is possible here,
it must always be in this cloud
and in this darkness.

Cloud, 1

Jesus is in the darkness

Jesus, you are both love and light,
and you are in the darkness
whether it brings pain or peace.
You are at work in my soul.
You move me to anguish
   with desire and longing
   for your light,
but as yet you do not allow me
   to rest in your love,
nor do you show me your light.
This state is darkness,
because you have hidden my soul
   from the false light of the world,
and yet I have not fully enjoyed
   the true light,
for I await the blessed love of my God
which my soul desires.

Hilton, *Ladder*, II, 24

God sends light as he pleases

Lord God, I find prayer hard and constraining.
I have little devotion,
but afterwards, with your help,
I will have devotion,
and it will become restful and easy for me,
though it was hard before.
Then I shall have very little labour,
    or none at all.
For then, Lord God,
you will work as you please;
not always,
not even for a long time together,
but as you please.
And it will seem a joyful thing for me
to leave you to do it.
Perhaps it will be your will
to send out a ray of spiritual light,
piercing this cloud of unknowing
    between you and me;
and you will show me some of your secrets
of which a person may not, or cannot, speak.
Then I shall feel my affection all aflame
    with the fire of your love,
far more than I know how to tell.

Cloud, 26

Your light in our night

Lord God, you give us faith as a light,
coming in nature from our endless day
   which is you, our Father God;
in which light our Mother, Christ,
   and our good Lord the Holy Spirit
lead us in this passing life.
You measure this light of faith
   with discretion,
and make it present to us
   in our need in the night.
Your light is the cause of our life,
the night is the cause of our pain
   and all our woe,
in which woe we deserve endless reward
   and thanks from our God,
for by your mercy and grace
we willingly know and believe you
   to be our light,
and we walk in your light
   wisely and mightily.
And at the end of woe,
suddenly you will open our eyes,
and in the clearness of sight
our light will be full,
which light is our God, our Creator, Father,
and the Holy Spirit,
in Christ Jesus our saviour.
So you show me and help me to understand
that our faith is our light in our night,
   which light is our God, our endless day.

Julian, *Showings*, 33

A night pregnant with good

Lord, the love of this world
   is false and transitory,
therefore I wish to abandon it,
   and seek your love.
I cannot at once experience your love.
   I must remain awhile in the night.
I cannot pass suddenly from one light to another,
   that is, from the love of this world
   to your perfect light, O God.
So let me withdraw my soul from earthly things
   into this night
by an intense desire
   to love, see, and know Jesus,
   and the things of the spirit.
This is a real night, for just as night is dark,
   hiding all created things
   and bringing bodily activity to a halt,
so when I set myself to think of you, Jesus,
and to desire your love alone,
I want you to withdraw
   my thoughts and affections
   from created things.
If you help me do this, it is night for me,
   and I am in darkness.
But this is a night pregnant with good,
   a glowing darkness,
for it shuts out the false love of the world,
and ushers in the dawn of your true day.
Indeed, the darker the night,
the nearer the true day of your love . . .
   for as the prophet says:
When I sit in darkness, the Lord is my light.

Hilton, *Ladder*, II, 24

Oil poured out

Your Name, O God, is like oil poured out.
For as long as my soul is sick
    and sore within,
burdened by the body,
saddened and disquieted
    by the perils and miseries of this life,
so long, O Lord God,
your name to me is not oil poured out,
    but sealed up.
But when my soul is suddenly flooded
    with the light of grace,
soothed and healed from all the filth of sin,
and when divine light and love
    brings spiritual strength
    and unspeakable joy,
then I can say with hearty praise
    and gladness of spirit:
'Your Name, O Lord, is oil poured out to me.'
For by your gracious visitation
the true significance of your Name
    is revealed to me,
that you are Jesus, Healing.
For your gracious presence alone
can raise me from sorrow
    and from sin.

Hilton, *Ladder*, II, 41

Turn reason into light

By itself knowledge is like water,
   tasteless and cold.
Lord Jesus, I offer this knowledge humbly to you,
   and ask for your grace.
Turn the water into wine with your blessing
   as you did at the request of your mother
   at the marriage feast.
By the gift of your Holy Spirit,
turn this savourless knowledge into wisdom,
and cold naked reason into spiritual light
   and burning love.

Hilton, *Ladder*, I, 4

Let me pierce the darkness

My God, it is my wish
to leave everything that I can think of
and choose for my love yourself,
the thing that I cannot think.
Because you can certainly be loved
     but not thought.
You can be taken and held by love
     but not by thought.
Therefore, though it is good at times, my God,
to think of your kindness and worthiness,
and though this is a light
     and a part of contemplation,
nevertheless in this exercise
     you want me to cast it down
and cover it over with a cloud of forgetting.
Let me step above it, stalwartly but lovingly,
and with devout, impulsive love,
     pleasing to you,
let me pierce that darkness above me.
Help me to smite upon that thick cloud of unknowing
     with a sharp dart of longing love.

Cloud, 6

Mary sat unmoving

Lord Jesus, teach me to be still and attentive
like Mary, who sat contemplating
    with all the love of her heart
the supreme and sovereign wisdom of your Godhead,
    clothed in the dark words of your manhood.
She had no desire to leave you,
not for anything that she saw
    or heard spoken around her.
But she sat unmoving,
sending up many a sweet and longing
    impulse of love,
to beat upon that high cloud of unknowing
    between her and her God.

Cloud, 17

Lord, you are our saviour and salvation

Our Lord, you tenderly teach us
and blessedly call us,
saying in our souls:
Leave me alone, my beloved child, attend to me,
I am enough for you.
So, Lord God,
help us to rejoice in you,
our saviour and our salvation.

Julian, *Showings*, 36

Draw up my love

Lord God, draw my love for you
  up to that cloud,
so that, through the help of your grace,
I may forget every other thing.

Cloud, 9

PRAYING THE PASSION

He fell on the ground, and prayed . . .

Sweet Lord Jesus Christ,
I thank you and am grateful to you
for that sweet prayer and that holy petition
which you made for us on Mount Olivet
before the holy passion.
I beg you, sweet Lord, to listen to my prayer.

Sweet Lord Jesus Christ,
I thank you and am grateful to you
for that great anxiety you had for us
when you became so full of distress
that an angel came from heaven to comfort you,
when you sweated blood in agony.
I ask you Lord,
and implore you, for your sweet mercy,
that you may be my help
in all my distress and my temptations;
and send me, Lord,
the angel of good counsel and comfort
in all my needs.

Rolle, *Meditations on the Passion*

They took him, and bound him

Sweet Jesus,
I thank you and am grateful to you
for the tortures and distresses
and disgraceful treatment and felonies
which people did to you entirely by betrayal.
They tied you up like a thief,
without compassion or sympathy.
Lord, I thank you for these sad, sweet steps
which you took for our love,
toward your own torment and your own death.
I ask you, Lord, and beg you
to untie us from the bonds of all our sins,
as you allowed yourself to be bound for love of us.

Rolle, *Meditations on the Passion*

Many bore false witness

I thank you, sweet Lord Jesus Christ,
for all injuries and tortures
and words of derision, malicious names and insults
which people directed at you and did to you
on that night in the harsh prison
where they held you captive.
Lord, I ask and implore you
that you send me patience and strength
to oppose without yielding
all the assaults and temptations of my opponents
and of my spiritual and physical enemies.

Rolle, *Meditations on the Passion*

They scourged him

Sweet Lord Jesus Christ,
I thank you for all the agonies
which you endured for us,
and for the sweet blood which you shed for us,
when you were so painfully beaten
and roped to the pillar.
I ask and beg you as my dear Lord,
for that sweet blood
which you bled so generously for me,
to be full deliverance for my soul.

Rolle, *Meditations on the Passion*

They plaited a crown of thorns

Sweet Lord Jesus Christ,
I thank you for being so covered in blood then,
so crowned with thorns
in the presence of all the people,
and your sweet face so spat on and so defiled.
Then on each side you were denounced and driven
and had the outcry raised against you
   for a violent death,
and you were condemned
   to the shameful death of hanging.
Blessed and thanked may you be for it.
I beg you, dear Lord,
that through your great compassion
you will give me grace and wisdom
to judge and criticise myself
so that my soul be saved.

Rolle, *Shorter Meditations*

He, bearing his cross, went out . . .

Sweet Lord Jesus Christ,
I thank you for the injuries and disgraces
which you endured so graciously and so gladly,
now by being tugged at,
now by being butted so disgracefully,
now by being struck,
now by being flogged so painfully and brutally;
and by carrying your own cross
   on your sweet, naked back,
like a thief carrying his own gallows
to be hanged on it himself at Mount Calvary,
where people gazed at wicked men and thieves,
deciding whether this one was a thief or a murderer:
and there you allowed them to put you on the cross.

Rolle, *Shorter Meditations*

His pains press my heart

Jesu to love may I be keen, you are my heavenly
   good.
Alas, my God, like a ruffian, is nailed on the rood.
His tender veins begin to burst, all running with
   blood;
Hands and feet with nails are fast: this changes all my
   mood.

Jesu, my King, to me is dear, who with his blood me
   bought:
Spread with spittle is his flesh clear, to death by
   beating brought;
For me he suffered pains severe: I am the wretch he
   wrought.
Therefore they press my heart most near; of them
   forget I nought.

Jesu, fortune of every fight, grace grant me to
   succeed,
That I may love you right, and have you as my meed.
Your love is firm through each tempting, there
   always at our need:
As you through grace are my yearning, in to your
   light me lead.

Rolle, *Lyrics*

The bright angels' bread

The thorn crowns my king; most deep is that
    pricking!
Alas, my joy, that sweet being is judged to the
    hanging.
Nailed were your hands, nailed were your feet,
And pierced was your side, so lovely and sweet.

Naked your white breast and red your bloody side;
Wan was your colour, your wounds deep and wide.
In five places on your flesh the blood down did slide
As streams do on the shore – such torture you can't
    hide.

Now contemplate great misery: how you are judged
    and dead
And nailed on to tree, the bright angels' bread.
Driven by men most cruel, you, my soul's good,
And defiled just like a fool, in heaven the holiest
    food.

A marvel then to see, if we all but understood,
How God in majesty was dying on the rood.
In truth it can be said, love dances first in ring,
What him so low has laid, if not love, was no thing.

Jesu, receive my heart, and to your love me bring;
My desire to you will dart: I long for your coming.
Make me now clean from sin, let love us ever join.
Kindle me fire within, that I your love may win
And see your face, Jesu: now let that bliss begin.

Jesu, my soul now mend: your love into me send,
That I with you life spend in joy that has no end.
In love wound now my thought, my heart lift up in
    glee;
My soul you dearly bought: make it your lover be.

Rolle, *Ego Dormio*

The last pain of your passion

Then I saw your sweet flesh drying before my eyes,
part after part drying up with astonishing pain.
And as long as there was any vital fluid
    in your flesh,
you went on suffering.
The long torment impressed me
as if you had been dead for a week,
    dying and on the point of death,
    always suffering this great pain.
Your sweet body was so discoloured,
    so dry, so shrivelled,
    so deathly and so pitiful
that it seemed to me
as if the greatest and the last pain
    of your Passion
was when your flesh dried up.

Julian, *Showings*, 16

92

Your body was full of wounds

Sweet Jesu!
Your body at that time was like heaven,
because just as heaven is full of stars,
so your body was full of wounds.
But your wounds, Lord, are better than the stars,
because stars only shine at night,
and your wounds are powerful by night and by day;
all the stars only give a little light at night,
and a single cloud can hide all of them;
but a single one of your wounds, sweet Jesu,
was and is sufficient to dispel the clouds of sin
and to clear the conscience of every sinful person.
Here, sweet Jesu,
I implore you that these wounds
may be my meditation night and day,
since in your wounds
lies the complete remedy for every disease
   of the soul.

Rolle, *Meditations on the Passion*

Your body is like a net

And again, sweet Jesu,
your body is like a net,
because just as a net is full of holes,
so your body is full of gashes.
Here, sweet Lord Jesu,
I implore you to catch me in the net
   of your flogging
so that all my feelings and love may be for you,
and draw me closer and closer to you,
and alongside you,
as a dragnet draws fish,
until I arrive at the bank of death,
so that no temptation,
no time of hardship nor time of prosperity
may ever tug me away from you;
and as a net draws fish ashore,
so, sweet Jesu, gather me up for your perfect joy.

Rolle, *Meditations on the Passion*

Your body is like a book

Sweet Jesu,
Your body is like a book
   entirely inscribed in red ink.
Now, sweet Jesu,
send me the grace to read this book
   again and again,
and to understand something of the sweetness
   of that reading;
and allow me the grace
to grasp something of the matchless love
   of Jesus Christ,
and to learn from that example
to love God in return as I should.

Rolle, *Meditations on the Passion*

Your body is like a meadow

Sweet Jesu:
Your body is like a meadow
full of scented flowers and health-giving herbs;
in just this way your body is full of wounds,
sweetly aromatic for a devout soul
and as health-giving as herbs for each sinful person.
Now, sweet Jesus, I implore you,
allow me the sweet aroma of mercy
and the health-giving medicinal prescription
    of grace.

Rolle, *Meditations on the Passion*

The greatest pain

Lord Jesus Christ,
this revelation of your pains,
fills me full of pains;
and then it came to me
that I had little known
what pain it was that I had asked,
and like a wretch I regretted it,
thinking that if I had known what it had been,
I should have been reluctant to ask for it.
For it seemed to me that my pains
 exceeded any mortal death.
I thought: 'Is there any pain in hell
 like this pain?'
And, Lord Jesus, you answered:
'Hell is a different pain, for in it there is despair.
But of all the pains that lead to salvation,
this is the greatest, to see your beloved suffer.'
How could any pain be greater
than to see you suffer,
my life, my bliss and all my joy?
Here I felt unshakably
that I love you, Lord Jesus Christ
so much more than myself
that there is no pain which can be suffered
like the sorrow which I feel to see you in pain.

Julian, *Showings*, 17

How much you love me!

How much you love me!
You loved me so much
   before you died for me,
that you wanted to die for me.
And now you have died for me,
and willingly suffered what you could.
And now all your bitter pain
and all your hard labour
is turned into everlasting joy and bliss
   for me and for you.
How could it now be
that I would pray to you
for anything pleasing to you
which you would not gladly grant to me?
For your delight is in my holiness
and in my endless joy and bliss in you.

Julian, *Showings*, 24

Jesus is my heaven

Lord, you taught me
to choose Jesus as my heaven,
whom I saw only in pain at that time.
No other heaven was more pleasing to me
than you, Jesus,
and you will be my bliss when I am there.
And this has always been a comfort to me,
that I chose you, Jesus, by your grace
to be my heaven
in all this time of suffering and of sorrow.
And so you taught me that I should always do so:
to choose you only to be my heaven,
in well-being and in woe.

Julian, *Showings*, 19

I am satisfied

Good Lord Jesus,
all my thanks to you;
good Lord Jesus, blessed may you be
because you suffered for me;
and it is a joy, a bliss and endless delight to you
that ever you suffered your Passion for me;
and if you could suffer more, you would suffer more.

Julian, *Showings*, 22

Jesu, son of God, Lord of Majesty

Jesu, son of God, Lord of Majesty,
Send to my heart the will you to desire solely.
Seize from me all love for this land so you my love
　　may be;
Take my heart into your hand: set me in stability.

Jesu, the Maiden's son, who with your love me
　　bought,
Pierce my soul with your spear which greatest love
　　to all has brought.
In longing, lead me to your light, firmly fix on you
　　my thought;
With your sweetness fill my heart, my cares away
　　be caught.

Wound my heart entire, control it at your command;
On enjoyment that endures firm make me fix my
　　mind.
May I your love secure; with grace my thoughts
　　expand,
Clean me from things impure, let me to you ascend.

Root it in my heart, that memory of your pain;
In sickness or unhurt, your love be ever mine.
My joy in you I see; receive my soul again.
My love all growing be, so it may ne'er decline.

My song is in sighing, while I live in this way:
My life is in longing, which binds me night and day,
Till I come to my King, where dwell with him I may,
And see his fair shining, in life that lasts for aye.

Rolle, 'A Song of Love Longing to Jesus', *Lyrics*

GOD WHO IS ALL

You are he who is all

You are he,
you are he.
You are he who is highest.
You are he whom I love.
You are he in whom I delight.
You are he whom I serve.
You are he for whom I long.
You are he whom I desire.
You are he whom I intend.
You are he who is all.

You are he, the power and goodness
   of fatherhood.
You are he, the wisdom and lovingness
   of motherhood.
You are he, the light and the grace
   which is all blessed love.
You are he, the Trinity.
You are he, the unity.
You are he, the supreme goodness
   of every kind of thing.
You are he who makes me to love.
You are he who makes me to long.
You are he, the endless fulfilling
   of all true desires.

Julian, *Showings*, 26, 59

How could anything be amiss?

Lord, you are God.
Lord, you are in all things.
Lord, you do all things.
You never remove your hands
   from your works,
nor ever will, without end.
You guide all things
to the end that you ordained them for,
   before time began,
with the same power
and wisdom and love
   with which you made them;
how could anything be amiss?

Julian, *Showings*, 11

God and man

Lord, may I know you and worship you
    as God and man,
and not as man only,
for you are both God and man,
and the whole reason why
    you are to be loved and worshipped
is that you are God
    who took the nature of man.
So I will adore you in my heart
and give you my love as God.
Let my mind worship you as Jesus,
    God in man,
    supreme Truth,
    supreme Goodness
    and blessed Life,
for so you are.

Hilton, *Ladder*, II, 30

Five great joys

Lord God, you rejoice
   that you are our Father.
Lord God, you rejoice
   that you are our Mother.
Lord God, you rejoice
   that you are our true Spouse,
and that our soul is your beloved wife.
Christ, you rejoice
   that you are our Brother,
Jesus, you rejoice
   that you are our Saviour.
These are five great joys
in which you want us to rejoice,
praising you, thanking you,
loving you,
endlessly blessing you.

Julian, *Showings*, 52

Our endless joy

God, you are Trinity:
Trinity is our maker,
Trinity is our protector,
Trinity is our everlasting lover,
Trinity is our endless joy
  and our bliss,
by our Lord Jesus Christ,
and in our Lord Jesus Christ:
  Blessed be our Lord!

Julian, *Showings*, 4

The Trinity

Lord God almighty,
in our making, you are our loving Father,
and God all wisdom, you are our loving Mother,
with the love and the goodness of the Holy Spirit
   which is all one God, one Lord.

And in the joining and the union
you are our very true spouse,
and we your beloved wife
and your fair maiden
with whom you are never displeased,
for you say:
   'I love you, and you love me,
   and our love will never divide in two.'

I contemplated your work, blessed Trinity,
in which contemplation I saw and understood
   these three properties:
the property of the fatherhood
and the property of the motherhood
and the property of lordship in one God.

Julian, *Showings*, 58

Father, Mother and Lord

Our great Father, almighty God,
you knew us and loved us before time began.
Out of this knowledge,
in your wonderful deep love,
by the prescient eternal counsel
  of all the blessed Trinity,
you wanted the second person
to become our Mother,
  our Brother and our Saviour.
From this it follows
that as truly as you, God, are our Father,
so truly are you our Mother.
Our Father wills,
our Mother works,
our good Lord the Holy Spirit confirms.
And therefore it is our part
to love you, our God,
  in whom we have our being,
reverently thanking and praising you
  for our creation,
mightily praying to you, our Mother,
  for mercy and pity,
and to our Lord the Holy Spirit
  for mercy and grace.

Julian, *Showings*, 59

Jesus, our true Mother

Jesus, by our first creation
   you are our true Mother in nature,
and by your taking our created nature
   you are our true Mother in grace.
All the lovely works
and all the sweet loving offices
   of beloved motherhood
are appropriated to you,
for in you we have this godly will,
whole and safe forever,
both in nature and in grace,
from your own goodness proper to you.

Julian, *Showings*, 59

Our courteous Mother

Our heavenly Mother Jesus,
often when you show us our falling
    and wretchedness,
we are so much afraid,
and so greatly ashamed,
that we scarcely know where we can
    put ourselves.
But you, our courteous Mother,
do not wish us to flee away,
for nothing would be less pleasing to you;
but you want us to be like a child.
For when it is distressed and frightened,
it runs quickly to its mother;
and if it can do no more,
it calls with all its might to its mother
    for help.
So you want us to act as a meek child, saying:
'My kind Mother,
my gracious Mother,
my beloved Mother,
have mercy on me.
I have made myself filthy and unlike you,
and I may not and cannot make it right
except with your help and grace.'

Julian, *Showings*, 61

113

You bear us for joy

Our great God,
the supreme wisdom of all things,
you arrayed and prepared yourself
    in this humble place,
all ready in our poor flesh
yourself to do the service
    and office of motherhood
    in everything.
The mother's service is nearest,
    readiest and surest:
nearest because it is most natural,
readiest because it is most loving,
and surest because it is most true.
No one might, or ever could,
    perform this office fully,
except you only, Lord.
Our mothers bear us for pain
    and for death,
But our true Mother Jesus,
you alone bear us for joy
    and for endless life.
Blessed may you be.

Julian, *Showings*, 60

114

Contemplating God's motherhood

Lord God,
I understand three ways of contemplating
   your motherhood.
The first is the foundation of
   our nature's creation;
the second is your taking of our nature,
where your motherhood of grace begins;
the third is your motherhood at work.
And in that, by your grace,
everything is penetrated,
in length and in breadth,
in height and in depth,
without end;
and it is all one love.

Julian, *Showings*, 59

You wrap and enfold us

Our good Lord,
you are everything that is good
and comforting for our help.
You are our clothing,
you wrap and enfold us for love,
    embrace and shelter us.
You surround us for your love,
which is so tender
that you may never desert us.
You are everything that is good.

Julian, *Showings*, 5

116

You are my healing

Lord, you are my salvation,
you are my God through grace,
and my healing.
You have bought me
and you have taken me up
from the toiling of this world to joy,
therefore I will never be moved from you.

Rolle, *Psalm 61*

Love was your meaning

Lord, you said:
'What, do you wish to know
    your Lord's meaning in this thing?'
And I know it well, Lord,
that love was your meaning.
Who reveals it to me?
    Love.
Why do you reveal it to me?
    For love.
Lord, let me remain in this,
and I will know more of the same.
But I will know no different,
    ever without end.

Julian, *Showings*, 86

You are Love

You are Love,
and all that you do is done out of love.
You are Jesus:
Might, Wisdom and holy Love.
You are God,
and you are Love.

Hilton, *Ladder*, II, 36

You are the Maker

You are Love,
and you are the Maker,
and everything which is made
endures, and will always endure,
because you love it;
and thus everything has being
through your love.

Julian, *Showings*, 5

BLESSINGS

True peace

I beseech almighty God
that true peace,
sane counsel,
and spiritual comfort in God,
with abundance of grace,
be always with you
and with all those on earth
    who love God.

Cloud, 75

With us constantly

His goodness never allows us
   to be alone;
may he be with us constantly
and tenderly excuse us,
and always protect us from blame
   in his sight.

Julian, *Showings*, 80

God make your soul wise

May God grant you grace and humility
  to make your soul wise,
and fire it with longing
  to see his face.

Hilton, *Ladder*, II, 46

God's cheerfulness

May you lead your life
    in light-heartedness;
keep hopelessness far away;
may gloom not remain with you,
but may God's cheerfulness
forever sing out merrily
    in your life.

Rolle, *Ghostly Gladness*

Sources

The prayers in this book are taken from the following full-length versions of the texts:

Julian of Norwich: Showings edited by Edmund Colledge and James Walsh, published in the Classics of Western Spirituality series by SPCK in the UK and by Paulist Press in the USA.
The Cloud of Unknowing edited by James Walsh, in the same series as above.
Richard Rolle: English Writings edited by Rosamund Allen, in the same series as above.
These three books are currently in print. Editions of Julian of Norwich, *The Cloud of Unknowing*, *The Ladder of Perfection* by Walter Hilton and *The Fire of Love* by Richard Rolle are also published by Penguin Classics.

The texts are available in the original Middle English in the following editions:
Julian of Norwich, *Revelations of Divine Love*, edited by Marion Glasscoe (Exeter Medieval Texts).
The Cloud of Unknowing and the Book of Privy Counselling, edited by Phyllis Hodgson (Early English Text Society, published by OUP).
The English Writings of Richard Rolle, Hermit of Hampole, edited by Hope Emily Allen (Oxford University Press, reissued by Alan Sutton Publishing).